THE EFFECT OF TOXIC LEADERSHIP

The culture of an organization is like a river. It can be fluid, strong and consistent, serving as lubricant while guiding its members in the right direction. In contrast a river can become stale and toxic, silently killing those who drink at its shore.[1]

—Ron Kaufman

We have all endured the bad boss or overbearing leader; however, toxic leaders are something more. According to J. Lipman-Blumen, "toxic leaders are those individuals who by dint of their destructive behaviors and dysfunctional personal qualities generate serious and enduring poisonous effects."[2] In short, toxic leaders damage organizations. When focusing on toxic leadership, many researchers emphasize the symptoms of toxicity (individual characteristics, traits) and not the disease (culture, climate, outcomes).[3] Several researchers agree that the long-term negative effect that toxic leaders have on an organization's culture and climate is a key variable in toxicity determination.[4] History shows that leaders have a major impact on the organization's they lead. According to T. Gilberson et al., "upper echelon leaders are believed to be the primary influence on the creation and development of organizational culture."[5] General George Washington and General Benedict Arnold were both effective leaders; however, their lasting effects on their organizations were profoundly different. Both leaders were as heroes of continental Army; however, one went on to become the father of our country and the other our most notorious traitor. According to Padilla et al., "If destructive leadership is defined in terms of harmful outcomes, then it is possible for 'good' leaders to produce bad outcomes, and bad leaders to produce desirable outcomes."[6] Toxic leaders abuse their power and position routinely, and invariably leave the organization worse than when they found it.[7] In other words, "Toxic leaders work to promote themselves at the expense of their subordinates …without considering the lasting ramifications to their unit, and the Army profession."[8] Although characteristics and traits may be helpful in identify toxic leaders, they fall short of a holistic view by failing to identify or discuss how an organization's culture may contribute to toxicity in its leaders.

Culture is a key strategic factor in predicting behaviors and outcomes. An organization's leadership and its culture are related elements of organizational life, because they directly and indirectly influence each other, and serve similar functions.[9] Broadly defined, an organization's culture is a relatively stable set of values, norms, and behaviors universally held by its members.[10] An organization's culture may have a moderating effect on the behavior of its members and may ultimately serve to promote toxic behavior. The Army's bureaucratic and authoritarian organizational structures tend to emphasize centralized decision-making, reward compliance and rely on standard operating procedures over employee innovation. As a result, "the institutionalized values and norms inherent in military organizations may facilitate the emergence of tyranny" and make them more susceptible to toxic leaders.[11] E. Schnider's theory of attraction-selection-attrition (ASA) suggests that senior leaders imbue an organization's culture with their own personal characteristics by establishing goals, values, and norms that attract people with similar personal characteristics.[12] Therefore, toxic leaders create toxic climates by changing the content of the culture.[13] The resulting damage to the organization's culture and climate may last for many years after the individual toxic leader has gone.

Toxic leadership is a topic of increasing interest in the military and civilian sectors. In this paper I will examine the cause and effect relationship between toxic leaders and the damaging cultures they foster. I will begin by defining toxic leadership; I will then use a classification-oriented approach to analyze the effect of toxic leadership on the elements of organizational culture: values, norms, and behaviors. Finally, I will explore the moderating environmental effects that may increase or mitigate the organization's vulnerability to the damage caused by toxic leaders. According to P. Senge, "the causes of many pressing public issues... lay in the very well-intentioned policies designed to alleviate them."[14] As Army leaders attempt to moderate toxic behavior, we must confirm that the cure does not kill the patient. By focusing on the ends with little regard for the means, and instituting policies designed to provide quick fixes, leaders may do irreparable harm to the culture and climate they are trying to protect. I will not make any suppositions about the individual characteristics or traits associated with toxic leaders; the intent of this paper is to add to the understanding of this significant organizational concern through initial conceptualization and theory.

Defining Toxic Leadership

According to R. Kaiser, R. Hogan, and S. Craig, "Every discussion of leadership depends on certain assumptions."[15] I will assume that toxic leadership is antithetical to good order and discipline and that the characteristics or traits displayed by toxic leaders result in serious negative effects for their employees.[16] The obvious next step for the strategic leader is to define toxic leadership in relationship to its effect on organizations. Kusy and Holloway suggest that toxic leaders have an "insidious effect...on organizational life and the welfare of both the organization and those who work diligently in pursuit of the organization's success."[17] Toxic leaders are inwardly motivated,

3

inherently destructive, and violate the legitimate interests of the organization. The harm that toxic leaders inflict extends beyond the organization's boundaries and directly influences the perception of stakeholders, customers, etc.[18] Kusy and Holloway refer to the toxic leader as the "tip of the toxic iceberg."[19] They suggest that the lasting human and financial costs of toxic leadership are "below the waterline" and that these effects do the most damage to organizations.[20] Toxic leadership is bad leadership that left unchecked compromises the organization's values and norms, and promotes noncompliant behaviors. If we agree that toxic leaders influence these variables negatively it becomes a strategic imperative to understand the distinct elements of these variables that are most susceptible, how toxic leaders affect them directly and indirectly, and explore methods to mitigate or eliminate these effects.

Toxic Leader Effect

Toxic leadership "harms people – and, eventually, the company as well."[21] Toxic leaders effect an organization's culture negatively by engaging in self-destructive behaviors that compromise his or her reputation and the values of the organization, or by failing to adhere to the normative standards of the organization, and underwriting or ignoring the noncompliance behavior of subordinates. To understand the effect that toxic leaders may have on organizations we must explore the different levels of an organization's culture. In this case, organizational values are ideas and beliefs about the kinds of objectives members of an organization should pursue and the appropriate methods or behaviors to achieve these objectives. From these organizational values we derive organizational norms, societal rules, and other guidelines that indicate appropriate kinds of behavior by members in certain situations and regulate the behavior of team members when interacting with one another.[22] Employees internalize

4

the norms and values of the organization and by extension the values of the leader. According to D. Lease, "Control through culture is so powerful because once these values are internalized; they become part of the individual's values, and the individual follows organizational values without thinking about them."[23] It is through the control of values, norms, and behaviors that toxic leaders damage organizations.

Values

Values are the basis for normalizing behaviors in organizations, and as such play a pivotal role in the ability of the toxic leader to inflict organizational damage. The Army is a values-based organization, and toxic leaders undermine organizational values by redefining the organization's goals and assigning importance to them. According to A. Reino and M Vadi, "Organizational values reflect the beliefs and understandings of individuals or groups about the means and ends of the organization."[24] Values are an enduring part of the organization's culture and helps define what the organization believes and how its members behave.[25] A review of the literature reveals a diverse set of opinions about the determinants of organizational values. Some authors suggest that the leader is the most important determinant, but others suggest that external forces have a more profound impact.[26] These external forces include: a) universal values, accepted by all members of a society; b) personal values, established by our individual experiences and interactions, guide how we relate to one another; and c) socio-cultural values, dominant values of the group or society that may change over time and may challenge personal values.[27] Assuming that a majority of the members of the society accept the universal values, it is difficult, although not impossible, for a single leader to corrupt them.[28] However, personal and socio-cultural values may be more context-driven and thereby more susceptible to toxic leader influence.[29]

In the Army, "organizations often take on the personality of their leaders."[30] After the battle of Kasserine Pass, during World War II, the morale and fighting spirit of the American II Corps was low.[31] General Eisenhower selected General George Patton, a bombastic armored corps officer to relieve General Lloyd Fredendall and breathe some life into the unit. General Patton believed that failure was not an option, and soon his unit believed it too. Leaders establish the core values and ethical guidelines that serve as the foundation for the organization. However, the employee's personal view of the world and the way he or she perceives their value in the organization plays a major role in espoused and expressed values. Results-oriented employees who value success and accomplishment may be more susceptible to the effects of toxic leaders. J. Steele noted that, "the impact that toxic leaders have on their subordinates' performance is greater for those who identify a strong sense of value and meaning in their jobs."[32] These negative impacts may be the result of acts committed by toxic leaders directly (e.g., unethical behavior, abuse), or actions omitted by the organization (e.g., failing to correct toxic behavior, or reinforce organizational values). Ultimately, when the members of the organization perceive a contradiction between the organization's values and the values of their leaders they have to choose which values to adopt. In a recent anecdotal example, five Army Soldiers were charged with murder in connection with the reported 'thrill killing' of several Afghan civilians. According to reports, the leader, an Army Staff Sergeant, "exploited a lawless platoon culture" to encourage others to go along with his plans and they eventually became willing and enthusiastic accomplices.[33] As toxic leaders advance and are rewarded for their achievements, subordinate leaders are incentivized to adopt their toxic values as a means of attaining power and promotion.

Research shows that incongruence between personal values and organizational values results in negative work attitudes and outcomes.[34] Selfless service is an Army core value, and leaders are expected to place the needs of their soldiers, and the organization above their own. However, toxic leaders tend to be self-serving and narcissistic, and tend to reward those members who support these tendencies. This behavior may result in a task or result-oriented value system that rewards the ends with no regard for the means used. The long-term result of this behavior may be a perception that the organization values results over processes and people. Worse, it may convince members of the organization that the institution lacks the will or the ability to root out problems, even when they diminish performance. The adjustment of organizational values is the toxic "gift that keeps right on giving." Once a toxic leader substitutes his or her values for the core values of the organization, a culture of toxicity forms until the organization applies corrective pressures. For example, General Stanley McChrystal, the senior U.S. commander in Afghanistan and members of his staff expressed their disparaging opinions of the current administration to a journalist.[35] This action is in direct violation of Army regulations and core values, and forced the President to relieve a valuable member of the organization to preserve good order and discipline. According to B. Seevers, "Values are neither completely stable nor unstable, but rather change in accordance to the…environments of the individuals and groups that embrace them."[36] As values weaken, norms of behavior also weaken.

Norms

One bad apple can spoil the whole bunch, and one toxic leader can redefine the norms of an organization. Norms are deeply rooted in the organization's culture, and reflect the attitudes of the team or group.[37] Shared norms develop within groups and

7

may be more susceptible to negative influences by leaders and members.[38] According to E. Harrison and J. Rosenzweig, "A norm is an idea in the minds of the members of a group…specifying what the members should do, ought to do, and are expected to do, under given circumstances."[39] Group norms provide security and predictability in the work environment.[40] Once a new group forms, the members share their assumptions and beliefs and reach consensus on how the group will interact internally and externally.[41] As new members enter the group, they receive instruction through some form of indoctrination or in processing on the accepted standards of behavior within the group.[42] Prescriptive norms define acceptable group behavior (e.g., punctuality), proscriptive norms define unacceptable group behavior (e.g., failing to complete readings), and descriptive norms define acceptable behavior in specific situations (e.g., acceptable response to a missed suspense).[43] According to S. Naumann, "Individuals use descriptive norms to ascertain behavior by using the heuristic 'If most people are doing this it must be the appropriate thing to do.'"[44]

Research suggests that the behavior of toxic leaders may serve to rationalize or excuse negative behavior in the group and establish a new 'toxic' set of norms.[45] K. Wilson-Starks stated that, "Some members may come to see toxic leadership as normal, and conform willingly. These will be groomed to be the next generation of toxic leaders."[46] Norms in the military are spelled out in regulations and standard operating procedures focused on standardizing the task or system at hand and less on the individuals or organization. This rational view of organizations assumes that the perfect system or set of regulations will render the perfect result regardless of the workers. In other words, if we build a perfect system based on the 'true nature' of the problem, we will in-turn develop a perfect workforce.[47] The underlying flaw of this theory is that it assumes that people are rational and will behave in an expected or prescribed manner.[48] In the Army, power resides at the senior levels and middle managers are task oriented, mission focused and concerned with results.[49] Mission success is the primary leader motivation and relationships are secondary. Leadership at the tactical level requires competencies designed to directly influence subordinates, and produce results. Participative forms of leadership are encouraged, but authoritative forms may be required as the situations change. FM 6-22 states that direct leadership consists of "providing clear and concise mission intent, and setting expectations for performance."[50] Commanders use local policies and procedures to regulate those areas not directed in higher guidance. Although members may establish norms of behavior within their groups, these norms are subject to the approval of the commander, and may be directly influenced by his or her negative behaviors. The requirement for good order and discipline, obedience to orders, and tactical control may make the cultural norms of military organizations more susceptible to the effect of toxic leaders. Shared norms such as treating each other with dignity and respect may not survive an abusive leader who encourages toxic behavior among his or her subordinate leaders. Military members rely on leaders to enforce rules and reinforce organization and group norms. Failure by leaders to execute this responsibility may lead to disparate behavior within the team and the corruption or wholesale rejection of established norms.[51] According to Stamper et al., "Behavior which is not governed by any kind of norms is, by definition, intrinsically chaotic or random."[52]

Reward allocation norms such as equity, equality, and responsibility establish how rewards and resources are distributed within the group. In the Army, resource allocation is a function of command and leadership. Healthy command climates are characterized as places where all employees believe they are valued for their contribution to the group. For example, if team members believe that their ideas and concerns are valued in the decision-making process they are more likely to buy-in to the final decision regardless as to whether or not their idea was accepted.[53] However, if team members perceive they are not valued they are more likely to withhold ideas, resist change, and be less productive.[54] Social justice within organizations refers to how employees perceive the level of fairness and equal treatment they receive from each other and the leadership.[55] Toxic leaders are by definition arbitrary in their application of punishments and rewards and contribute to increasing feelings of injustice among employees.[56] The group-value model put forth by E. Lind and T. Tyler suggests that employee's value fairness from leaders and peers because it indicates acceptance within the group.[57] Military members rely on one another for not only routine mission success but also life or death in combat. If members of the organization perceive that they are not valued or are treated unfairly they are more likely to disengage or feel alienated within the team. A positive culture is based on positive shared norms. Teams use norms to secure the group against chaotic behavior, increase efficiency, and distinguish themselves from other groups and most important foster trust by outlining acceptable behavior.[58] In the Army, trust is the holy grail of leadership and is essential for teamwork. According to P. Lencioni "trust is the confidence among team members that their peers' intentions are good, and that there is no reason to be protective or careful around the group."[59] Toxic leaders exhibit hostile and abusive behaviors, demonstrate a complete disregard for subordinates, and lead through iron-fisted control.[60] These behaviors are detrimental to building team trust and ultimately damage the organization and its culture by redefining the way members interact and behave toward one another.

<u>Behaviors</u>

Values and norms are intangible representations of what the leaders and members of a team think they should be, know, and do (goals); however, behaviors are the visible manifestation of what the organization believes and values (actions).[61] According to B. Tepper et al., "subordinates who perceive that their supervisors are more abusive are less satisfied with their jobs…and less willing to perform pro-social organizational behaviors."[62] Pro-social behaviors such as initiative, helping, and loyalty are examples of citizenship or compliance behaviors.[63] However, antisocial behaviors such as obstruction or resistance to authority are examples of noncompliance.[64] Compliance behaviors extend beyond job description and encompass those voluntary behaviors that promote teamwork and effective administration of the organization. The Army is a hierarchical organization by design; however, members are encouraged to 'take the initiative' and exceed standards or perform duties outside their duty description for the good of the unit. Initiative behavior in organizations requires commitment from the employees to the mission and from the leadership to the employees.[65] Toxic leaders fail to inspire initiative in organizations – alternately, they inspire the wrong kind of initiative. They may over-control or micro-manage teams and discourage individual initiative, or they establish an environment that encourages destructive actions in subordinates.[66] As toxic leadership begins to degrade the values and trust inherent in the organization's culture, acts of employee abuse or harassment may increase.[67] Harassing behaviors may include hazing, ostracism, disparaging statements, threats, and in extreme cases physical violence.[68] According to General M. Dempsey, Chairman of the Joint Chiefs of Staff, incidents of hazing and bullying "undermine our values, tarnish our profession, and erode the trust that bonds us."[69] Workplace harassment can have serious effects on employee morale, and job satisfaction by creating a toxic culture that rewards bullying or mobbing behaviors and devalues civility and mutual respect.[70] In 2010, three Army noncommissioned officers were found guilty of cruelty and maltreatment of Soldiers in Iraq after one member of the platoon committed suicide. Prosecutors claimed that these Soldiers "established a pattern of cruelty and mistreatment" by targeting Soldiers for ridicule, arbitrary punishments, and physical abuse.[71] Abusive behaviors may become ingrained in the organization's culture as they are practiced and encouraged by the leadership.

According to Kusy and Holloway, negative behaviors trigger a negative response and "soon the triggers and the reactions begin to damage the team or individuals, who may react in ways that reinforce the toxic behaviors."[72] Organizational corruption behaviors manifest as a "willful perversion of order, ideals, and perhaps most important, trust - a 'moral deterioration.'"[73] Mutual trust is developed through positive interaction and experiences, as team members interact they become less guarded and more amenable to sharing and collaboration. Self-interest and office politics can erode or inhibit trust between team members and cause dysfunction.[74] Organizational corruption extends beyond the behaviors and traits of individuals and encompasses the effect that corrupt acts have on the group, unit, or organization. Left unchecked these actions can spread to other areas of the organization and amplify the scope of the problem in ways that threaten the culture and climate of the organization, and lead to increased instances of deviant social behavior.[75] According to L. Bolton and M. Grawitch, workplace deviance is a "voluntary behavior…that violates significant organizational norms and in doing so threatens the well-being of the organization, its members, or both."[76] Incidents of workplace deviance may include sexual harassment, antisocial behavior, or workplace conflict.[77] Although not all incidents of workplace deviance occur because of toxic leadership, retaliation against the organization or individuals is frequently the response to negative experiences in the workplace.[78]

Toxic leaders are likely to be associated with increases in unethical behavior and organizational corruption among both leaders and subordinates.[79] Strategic leaders must be mindful of not only the short-term 'tactical' impact of their behavior, but also must consider the enduring 'strategic' implications for the organization. According to J.P. Steele, "Toxic leadership in the Army can lead to mutiny and death as well as a whole host of relatively less serious but still troubling outcomes."[80] Many times the first indication of a toxic culture or climate is the noncompliance behavior of the organization's members.[81] Toxic leaders survive by disguising their behavior and producing results for the organization, at least in the short-term. Unfortunately, for the organization, by the time the true nature of the toxic behavior manifests the organizational damage is widespread. According to Kusy and Holloway, "recognizing that you have a toxicity problem in your team or group means understanding that complaints to you may not be consistent with your impression."[82] Toxic leaders do not occur spontaneously, they require a culture and system to sustain and empower them.[83]

The Army has a distinct set of values and norms that outline acceptable behavior and are the key building blocks of an organization's culture. According to B. Seevers, "culture defines expectations."[84] Toxic leadership damages organizations by "poisoning enthusiasm, creativity, autonomy, and innovative expression. Toxic leaders disseminate their poison through over-control."[85] The military's centralized structure may contribute to the emergence of toxic leaders by valuing results more than processes and relationships. A centralized structure reserves control or 'power' to the leader, and thus hinders the ability to identify or implement change at the lowest level. This may promote the perception among subordinates that they are not valued members of the team and lead to negative behavior and outcomes.[86] The sign of a healthy command climate and organizational culture is "congruence between the organization's values and the behavior of members."[87] Although an organization's culture is important, an organization response to toxic behavior may have a moderating effect on the degree of damage caused by toxic leaders.

Moderating Effects

Research suggests that an organization's culture may have a moderating effect on the influence of toxic leaders.[88] An organization's response to a toxic leader or toxic environment sends a clear message about what the organization values. According to G. McNeal, "Organizational culture is seen as a social energy that moves people to act... culture is to the organization what personality is to the individual."[89] Cultures are resilient and resistant to change; however, in a favorable climate, toxic subcultures not only form, but also thrive. How do organizations become a toxic life support system? A review of the literature reveals three ways that organizations may promote a culture of toxicity. First, through migration, which consists of changes in structure or work

14

assignments designed to accommodate a toxic person. Second, through enabling or overlooking negative behaviors to retain a productive toxic person. Finally, through a lack of internal governance, which results in a failure to place limits on power or to recognize toxic behavior in subordinates.[90] Bad leadership and toxic leaders exist in organizations throughout the world, and although leaders may not intentionally promote toxic behavior, a failure to observe and moderate the organization's culture may result in new toxic culture. Organizations in which migration is easy, or that enable toxic behaviors, or that fail to govern effectively, are going to suffer higher incidence of toxic leadership and be more susceptible to its effects.

Migration

In a national survey of toxic personalities, respondents indicated that they believe that "organizations contribute to the toxic person getting away with counterproductive behaviors."[91] One way that toxic leaders escape detection is by hiding in plain sight. The Army is inherently bureaucratic and the personnel systems are incomprehensible at best. The process to relieve or fire a toxic leader can take months and in some cases years. According to Kusy and Holloway organizations may use restructuring as intervention technique in dealing with toxic people.[92] They suggest that, "restructuring is often code for…I don't know how to handle this person."[93] Screw up and move up is an age-old military maxim, which implies that if a person fails or causes trouble the organization will reassign him or her to relieve the immediate problem. It is often easier for an organization's leadership to 'relocate' or send a toxic person to school than it is to document his or her behavior and eliminate him or her. In the case of senior leaders who violate organizational values or norms of behavior, their superiors must exercise the personal courage needed to correct or eliminate the problem. In 1997, General

Ralston was a top candidate for Chairman of the Joint Chiefs of Staff; however, during the vetting process reporters discovered allegations of a prior adulterous affair. Although the allegations effectively derailed General Ralston's chances of appointment, in 2000, he became the Supreme Allied Commander for the North Atlantic Treaty Organization (NATO). When asked about the perception of a double standard, General M. Dugan, former Air Force Chief of Staff, stated "I oppose adultery – I don't oppose adulterers...but in this case or every case...the 'don't ask don't tell' philosophy has been applied for years."[94] The migration of toxicity within the organization only serves to promulgate negative behavior, in favor of a shortsighted sense of relief. Toxic leaders may also use migration techniques to remove members of the organization that do not conform to their toxic agenda.

The practice of toxic migration is particularly damaging to organizations because the leadership recognizes that there is a toxic situation and is not only willing to let it continue, but is also willing to burden another organization with a known liability. This willingness does not originate from a sense of loyalty to the toxic person, but from frustration in having to deal with them and a desire to eliminate the pain associated with them. B. Kellerman describes this type of leadership as insular and suggests that these leaders will "minimize or disregard the health and welfare of the 'other,' this is, of those outside the group or organization for which they are directly responsible."[95] Insular leaders may operate from a desire to preserve the integrity of their organization at any cost, and that final cost may be delivering another organization into the hands of a known toxic leader. Although this type of leadership behavior may garner approval from the members of the 'protected' group, this type of toxic culture may result "in negative organizational outcomes that compromise the quality of life for all constituents."[96]

Enabling

Toxic leaders thrive in toxic systems because these systems enable toxic behavior.[97] The toxic triangle as described by A. Padilla et al., suggests that the toxic system is made up of not only destructive leaders, but also "susceptible followers and conducive environments."[98] S. Rickless describes enabling harm as "withdrawing an obstacle that would, if left in place, prevent a pre-existing causal sequence from leading to foreseen harm."[99] Many researchers suggest that the organization should focus on those senior leaders who enable the toxic leaders under their control.[100] According to the equivalence hypothesis, enabling harm is the moral equivalent of allowing harm.[101] In other words, by doing nothing to stop or prevent toxic behavior organizations develop a culture that allows, and in some cases encourages toxic behavior. Toxic leaders produce negative consequences for their followers and organizations. So how do they remain in positions of leadership? Simply put, they produce results. Although it can be argued that these results are short-lived and ultimately damaging to the organization, nonetheless they are results. In an effort to achieve a desired result, organizations and followers may tolerate a toxic leader and the effect he or she may have on the organization.[102] According to Kusy and Holloway, "It is very difficult to deal with toxic people when they are good producers."[103] An abusive leader whose unit scores highest on the physical fitness test, and excels during gunnery may be excused for his abusive behavior because these visible results make the organization look good. In this case, the organization values the ends more than the means. Organizations enable toxic behavior by not intervening to stop it, or by underwriting it. These leaders routinely "run

17

interference for the toxic individual, and provide stepping stones to help him or her be even more productive."[104]

What is the role of followers in enabling toxic leaders? According to W. Bennis, "followers play a vital role in the presence of toxic leaders."[105] He contends that followers have the moral duty to remove toxic leaders from their ranks, and that without the willing support of followers' these destructive leaders would be powerless. However, some researchers suggest that followers may enable or tolerate toxic behavior in leaders to achieve their own goals and objectives.[106] The military is a hierarchical organization, for subordinates to band together to remove a leader is unlikely, and in some cases mutinous. However, personal courage is an espoused Army value and as "followers bear the brunt of the horrors toxic leaders make," this would suggest a need for followers to make the case for change without disrupting the organization's structure.[107] Here again the organization has a major role to play in deterring toxic leadership. Army units use commander open door policies and the inspector general to provide subordinates a venue to address concerns with the command directly. One concern with these options may be the requirement to discuss concerns with a member of the chain of command first or seek permission from a supervisor before addressing them to the commander. The idea behind this requirement is often the desire to 'handle problems at the lowest level' and reinforce the chain of command; however, in some cases this requirement may intimidate subordinates and deter reporting. How do organizations support the chain of command while at the same time providing subordinates with avenues to report abuses? Whistle-blowing activities are outwardly encouraged as a means to expose criminal or toxic behavior in the organization;

however, "voicing outside the organization is, in most cases, a violation of the organization's norms."[108] Enabling organizations lack sufficient mechanisms to provide subordinates with opportunities to give leaders feedback or in extreme cases seek redress at higher levels. How effective would Hitler or Stalin have been if their circle of followers had refused to enable their behavior?

Leaders are encouraged to know themselves and seek self-improvement. A self-aware leader understands his or her strengths and weaknesses and uses feedback from subordinates and superiors to improve performance and leadership style.[109] Whether or not a leader will be effective depends on how he or she perceives their role in the organization, and their understanding of the organization's climate and culture. Unfortunately, some leaders are not receptive to feedback and discount the ability of subordinates to provide a true assessment of leaders. Junior Soldiers may not be equipped to provide insights into the intricacies of command; however, they are more than capable of informing leaders about how they perceive the way they are being treated. Does the Army culture value the opinions of subordinates, and if not, with declining budgets and reduced work force requirements how long will subordinates tolerate a toxic culture?

Governance

In the Army, senior leaders exercise command and control through subordinate leaders. Organizational governance outlines the relationship between leaders and subordinates.[110] According to H. Tarraf, governance is an agency's response to the "problems created by the separation of ownership and control" and encompasses the organization's rules and constraints on decision-making.[111] Effective governance forms a balance between what leaders and subordinates want and properly incentivize leaders to work toward the best interest of the organization. It also ensures that senior leaders are kept informed about the actions taken by subordinate leaders. Effective leaders look beyond the outward displays of good units and look below the surface to determine the true nature of the organization's culture. Army leadership studies conducted in 2009 and 2010 reveal that more than 80% of survey respondents encountered toxic leaders within the last year.[112] Rooting out toxic leadership takes time and effort. According to A. Padilla et al., "destructive leadership is most likely in senior jobs where there is less supervision."[113] Often subordinate leaders do not want to 'air dirty laundry' and may decide to suffer in silence. Because of misplaced loyalty, senior leaders may not be aware of a toxic person's behavior. One reason for this may be "that organizations are running flatter and leaner, with fewer management structures in place to coral bullies."[114] Another reason for leaders not being aware of toxic behavior may be that he or she does not consider the behavior toxic. Army leaders are a product of their environment, unlike corporations that hire mid-level and senior level managers to guide their organizations; the Army must assess, develop, and prepare its leaders at all levels. There are no 'Leader's-R-Us' outlets to support the Army mission and therefore in some instances obliviousness to toxic behavior may be the result of worldview. If the statistics on toxic leadership in the Army are true, then they are not only present in the ranks, but we are also assessing, and promoting them.

Hierarchy and bureaucracy are behavioral artifacts ingrained in the military culture; however, after 10 years of persistent conflict the time may be right to explore new paradigms. Given the potential damage that toxic leaders have on organizations culture and climate, one has to wonder why regulations and procedures sometimes fail to prevent toxic behavior. These failures in governance may contribute to toxic leadership. As a culture, the Army is passionate about leadership. Countless studies, books, and research projects are dedicated to understanding and improving the art of leadership. One reason for this preoccupation is the cost of failure. Leadership failures cost resources, and lives. Military leaders wield almost total control of their organizations. Commanders are both judge and jury in some cases, and centralized command is a prerequisite for good order and discipline in the military. Commanders are responsible and accountable for everything their organizations do or fail to do. However, does centralizing power in this manner lead to abuses and toxicity? According to Edmund Burke, "Power, in whatever hands, is rarely guilty of too strict limitations on itself."[115] The U.S. Government is strengthened by a system of checks and balances in which no one person or branch of government may assume absolute power. According to A. Padilla et al., a leader's discretion "concerns the degree to which managers are free from institutional constraints."[116] This freedom to act without interference is an essential element of the chain of command and is founded on the trust and confidence we have in our leaders. However, does this freedom make the organization more susceptible to toxic leadership and abuse?

Centralized governance systems that concentrate power and decision making at the top of the organization may promote a culture of reliance and indifference among subordinates.[117] A shared leadership perspective focuses less on formal structures and hierarchies and more on preparing members to assume leadership roles in the organization. According to C. Pearce et al., "Shared leadership occurs when group members actively and intentionally shift the role of leader to one another as necessitated by the environment or circumstances in which the group operates."[118] In short, it is the role of the organization to provide an environment suitable for learning and growth, and it is the role of the members to effect change through innovative and adaptive thinking. It is difficult for toxic leaders to succeed in organizations with effective forms of governance that include appropriate checks and balances on the behavior of leader, and avenues for subordinates to provide feedback to senior leaders.

Conclusion

Toxic leadership damages the organization's culture by violating the legitimate interests of the organization and decreasing the commitment and motivation of its members. The negative outcomes caused by toxic leaders create lasting and enduring harm to the organization's culture and climate. Every organization has a distinct culture that sets it apart and guides everything that its members do. Culture influences the way individuals feel about the organization, and how they react to one another. How an organization reacts to or takes steps to prevent the effects toxic leadership may have a direct impact on the degree of damage. By regulating moderating behaviors and improving methods of organizational governance, Army leaders may reduce incidents of out-of-value behavior by members of the organization, and reduce or eliminate toxic behavior among leaders and subordinates.

Endnotes

[1] Brenda Bertrand, "Transformation within Organizational Culture" http://www.leadingtoday.org/weleadinlearning/bb-oct02.htm.

[2] Jean Lipman-Blumen, "Toxic Leadership: When Grand Illusions Masquerade as Noble Visions," *Leader to Leader* 2005, no. 36 (2005): 29.

[3] Melissa A. Fitzpatrick, "Oh No! The Boss Has Gone "Psycho!"," *Nursing Management*2000; Gillian Flynn, "Stop Toxic Managers before They Stop You!," *Workforce* 78, no. 8 (1999); John. D. Genio, "The Toxic Boss," *Armed Forces Comptroller* 47, no. 1 (2002); Warren Wright, "The Leadership Detox Diet," *Training Journal*, (2009).

[4] M. Kusy and E. Holloway, *Toxic Workplace!: Managing Toxic Personalities and Their Systems of Power* (San Francisco, CA: Jossey-Bass, 2009); Christian Thoroughgood, Samuel Hunter, and Katina Sawyer, *Bad Apples, Bad Barrels, and Broken Followers? An Empirical Examination of Contextual Influences on Follower Perceptions and Reactions to Aversive Leadership* (Springer Science & Business Media B.V., 2011), Report, 01674544.

[5] Tomas Giberson and others, "Leadership and Organizational Culture: Linking Ceo Characteristics to Cultural Values," *Journal of Business & Psychology* 24, no. 2 (2009): 125.

[6] A. Padilla, Hogan, R., & Kaiser, R., "The Toxic Triangle: Destructive Leaders, Susceptible Followers, and Conducive Environments," *The Leadership Quarterly* 18, no. 3 (2007): 178.

[7] Blake E. Ashforth, "Petty Tyranny in Organizations: A Preliminary Examination of Antecedents and Consequences," *Revue Canadienne des Sciences de l'Administration/Canadian Journal of Administrative Sciences* 14, no. 2 (1997); Bennett J. Tepper, "Consequences of Abusive Supervision," *Academy of Management Journal* 43, no. 2 (2000).

[8] J. P. Steele, *Antecedents and Consequences of Toxic Leadership in the U.S. Army: A Two Year Review and Recommend Solutions* (Fort Leavenworth, KS: Center for Army Leadership, 2011), 3, CAL Technical Report 2011-3.

[9] E.H. Schein, "Culture: The Missing Concept in Organization Studies," *Administrative Science Quarterly* 41, no. 2 (1996).

[10] Bernard Lim, "Examining the Organizational Culture and Organizational Performance Link: A Critical Review of the Methodologies and Finding of Recent Researchers into the Presumed Link between Culture and Performance," *Leadership & Organization Development Journal* 16, no. 5 (1995).

[11] Ashforth: 128.

[12] Benjamin Schneider, Harold W. Goldstein, and D. Brent Smith, "The Asa Framework: An Update," *Personnel Psychology* 48, no. 4 (1995).

[13] Giberson and others.

[14] Peter M. Senge, *The Fifth Discipline : The Art and Practice of the Learning Organization*, Rev. and updated. ed. (New York: Doubleday/Currency, 2006), 14.

[15] Robert B. Kaiser, Robert Hogan, and S. Bartholomew Craig, "Leadership and the Fate of Organizations," *American Psychologist* 63, no. 2 (2008): 96.

[16] Kusy and Holloway; M. Van Vugt, Hogan, R., & Kaiser, R. B., "Leadership, Followership, and Evolution: Some Lessons from the Past," *American Psychologist* 63, no. 3 (2008).

[17] Kusy and Holloway, 10.

[18] A. Goldman, "High Toxicity Leadership: Borderline Personality Disorder and the Dysfunctional Organization," *Journal of Managerial Psychology* 21, no. 8 (2006).

[19] Kusy and Holloway, 12.

[20] Ibid., 19.

[21] Karen Wilson-Starks, "Toxic Leadership," (2003). http://www.transleadership.com/ToxicLeadership.pdf (accessed December 21, 2011).

[22] Kaiser, Hogan, and Craig; Lim.

[23] David Lease, "From Great to Ghastly: How Toxic Organizational Cultures Poison Companies the Rise and Fall of Enron, Worldcom, Healthsouth, and Tyco International," (Norwich University, 2006), 27.

[24] Anne Reino and Maaja Vadi, "What Factors Predict the Values of an Organization and How?," *University of Tartu - Faculty of Economics & Business Administration Working Paper Series*, no. 71 (2010): 5.

[25] Brenda Seevers, "Identifying and Clarifying Organizational Values," *Journal of Agricultural Education* 41, no. 3 (2000).

[26] Lim; Edgar H. Schein, *Organizational Culture and Leadership*, 3rd ed., The Jossey-Bass Business & Management Series (San Francisco: Jossey-Bass, 2004).

[27] Vytautas Boguslauskas and Goda Kvedaraviciene, "Difficulties in Identifying Company's Core Competencies and Core Processes," *Engineering Economics* 62, no. 2 (2009); J. J. Illies, & Reiter-Palmon, R, "Responding Destructively in Leadership Situations: The Role of Personal Values and Problem Construction," *Journal of Business Ethics* 82, no. 1 (2008); Seevers.

[28] Seevers.

[29] Steven H. Appelbaum and Barbara T. Shapiro, "Diagnosis and Remedies for Deviant Workplace Behaviors," *Journal of American Academy of Business, Cambridge* 9, no. 2 (2006); Sasha Grant, "A Legacy of Charismatic Leadership: An Examination of Individual, Social, and Organizational Identification," *Conference Papers -- International Communication Association*, (2009).

[30] U.S. Department of the Army, *Army Leadership: Competent, Confident, and Agile*, Field Manual 6-22 (Washington, D.C.: U.S. Department of the Army, October 2006), 2-3.

[31] George S. Patton and Paul D. Harkins, *War as I Knew It* (Boston: Houghton Mifflin Co., 1995).

[32] Steele, 2.

[33] Jeremy B. White, "Trial Begins for Alleged Ringleader of 'Kill Team' That Murdered Afghanistan Civilians," *New York International Business Times US*.November 1, 2011

[34] Barry Posner, "Another Look at the Impact of Personal and Organizational Values Congruency," *Journal of Business Ethics* 97, no. 4 (2010).

[35] Anne Gearan, "Mcchrystal Says He'll Retire," *Army Times* (June 29, 2012). http://www.armytimes.com/news/2010/06/ap_mcchrystal_retire_062810/.

[36] Seevers: 71.

[37] Giberson and others.

[38] Ashforth: 16.

[39] E. Frank Harrison and James E. Rosenzweig, "Professional Norms and Organizational Goals: An Illusory Dichotomy," *California Management Review* 14, no. 3 (1972): 39.

[40] Stefanie E. Naumann, "The Effects of Norms and Self-Monitoring on Helping Behavior," *Journal of Behavioral Studies in Business* 2, (2010).

[41] Ronald Stamper and others, "Understanding the Roles of Signs and Norms in Organizations," *Journal of Behavior & Information Technology* 19, no. 1 (2000).

[42] Ibid.

[43] Naumann.

[44] Ibid.: 2.

[45] Lamarcus Bolton and Matthew J. Grawitch, *When Good Employees Go Bad: How Organizations May Be Facilitating Workplace Deviance*, vol. 5 (Washington, District of Columbia, US: American Psychological Association (APA), Practice Directorate, 2011); Rosa R. Krausz, "Comments On "Business as Usual?: Ethics in the Fast-Changing and Complex World of Organizations"," *Transactional Analysis Journal* 41, no. 2 (2011); James K. Summers and others, "Dysfunctional Executive Behavior: What Can Organizations Do?," *Business Horizons* 53, (2010).

[46] Wilson-Starks.

[47] M. Addleson, "Resolving the Spirit and Substance of Organizational Learning," *Journal of Organizational Change Management* 9, no. 4/5 (1996).

[48] Gareth R. Jones, *Organizational Theory, Design, and Change*, 6th ed. (Upper Saddle River, N.J.: Prentice Hall, 2010).

[49] François Maon, Adam Lindgreen, and Valérie Swaen, "Thinking of the Organization as a System: The Role of Managerial Perceptions in Developing a Corporate Social Responsibility Strategic Agenda," *Systems Research & Behavioral Science* 25, no. 3 (2008): 413.

[50] U.S. Department of the Army, 3-7.

[51] Mark Levine and Scott Sibary, "Workplace Teams: Ethical and Legal Concerns and Approaches," *Ethics & Behavior* 11, no. 1 (2001).

[52] Stamper and others.

[53] Andrew C. Boynton and Bill Fischer, *Virtuoso Teams : Lessons from Teams That Changed Their Worlds* (Harlow, England ; New York: FT Prentice Hall, 2005); Glenn M. Parker, *Team Players and Team Work : New Strategies for Developing Successful Collaboration*, 2nd ed. (San Francisco, CA: Jossey-Bass, 2008).

[54] Leigh L. Thompson, *Making the Team : A Guide for Managers*, 3rd ed. (Upper Saddle River, NJ: Pearson/Prentice Hall, 2008).

[55] Tuija Seppälä, Jukka Lipponen, and Anna-Maija Pirttilä-Backman, "Leader Fairness and Employees' Trust in Coworkers: The Moderating Role of Leader Group Prototypicality," *Group Dynamics: Theory, Research, and Practice*, (2012).

[56] A. Goldman, *Transforming Toxic Leaders* (Stanford, CA: Stanford Business Books/Stanford University Press, 2009); M. Kusy, & Holloway, E., *Toxic Workplace!: Managing Toxic Personalities and Their Systems of Power* (San Francisco, CA: Jossey-Bass, 2009).

[57] E. Allan Lind and Tom R. Tyler, *The Social Psychology of Procedural Justice*, Critical Issues in Social Justice (New York: Plenum Press, 1988).

[58] Parker.

[59] Patrick Lencioni, *The Five Dysfunctions of a Team : A Leadership Fable*, 1st ed. (San Francisco: Jossey-Bass, 2002), 195.

[60] George G. Bloomer, *Authority Abusers : Toxic Leadership and Its Effects in Homes, Churches, and Relationships*, Rev. and expanded ed. (New Kensington, PA: Whitaker House, 2008); Clive Boddy, *Corporate Psychopaths, Bullying and Unfair Supervision in the Workplace* (Springer Science & Business Media B.V., 2011), Report, 01674544; Thoroughgood, Hunter, and Sawyer.

[61] Lim.

[62] Bennett J. Tepper and others, "Procedural Injustice, Victim Precipitation, and Abusive Supervision," *Personnel Psychology* 59, no. 1 (2006).

[63] Jeff Joireman and others, "A Social Dilemma Analysis of Organizational Citizenship Behaviors," in *Working Papers Series* (Hyderabad, India: Indian School of Business, 2005).

[64] Ibid.

[65] J Martin, *Culture in Organizations: Three Perspectives* (New York, NY: Oxford University Press, 1992).

[66] Flynn; Wilson-Starks.

[67] Thoroughgood, Hunter, and Sawyer.

[68] Goldman, "High Toxicity Leadership: Borderline Personality Disorder and the Dysfunctional Organization."

[69] Donna Miles and Tyrone Marshall, "Dempsey: Hazing, Bullying 'Intolerable' in Military" http://www.army.mil/article/71315/Dempsey__Hazing__bullying__intolerable__in_military/ (accessed February 20, 2012).

[70] Steven H. Lopez, Randy Hodson, and Vincent J. Roscigno, "Power, Status, and Abuse at Work: General and Sexual Harassment Compared," *Sociological Quarterly* 50, no. 1 (2009).

[71] Aamer Madhani, "Court-Martial Weighed in Iraq Discipline Cases" http://www.armytimes.com/news/2009/10/gns_court_martial_iraq_discipline_101209/ (accessed February 20, 2012).

[72] Kusy and Holloway, *Toxic Workplace!: Managing Toxic Personalities and Their Systems of Power*, 10.

[73] Blake E. Ashforth and others, "Re-Viewing Organizational Corruption," *Academy of Management Review* 33, no. 3 (2008): 671.

[74] P Lencioni, *The Five Dysfunctions of a Team: A Leadership Fable* (San Francisco, CA: Jossey-Bass, 2002).

[75] Ashforth and others, "Re-Viewing Organizational Corruption."

[76] Bolton and Grawitch, np.

[77] Randi Sims, "A Study of Deviance as a Retaliatory Response to Organizational Power," *Journal of Business Ethics* 92, no. 4 (2010).

[78] Bolton and Grawitch.

[79] Alan A. Cavaiola and Neil J. Lavender, *Toxic Coworkers : How to Deal with Dysfunctional People on the Job* (Oakland, Calif.: New Harbinger Publications, 2000); Alan Goldman, *Transforming Toxic Leaders* (Stanford, Calif.: Stanford Business Books/Stanford University Press, 2009).

[80] Steele, 2.

[81] Kusy and Holloway, *Toxic Workplace!: Managing Toxic Personalities and Their Systems of Power*.

[82] Ibid., 22.

[83] Ibid.

[84] Seevers: 71.

[85] Wilson-Starks, "Toxic Leadership," (2003).

[86] Zoran Lovrekovic and Enes Sukic, "Information Technologies Do Not Solve Problems in Business -- They Just Provide Solutions If Used in the Right Way," *TTEM- Technics Technologies Education Management* 6, no. 3 (2011).

[87] Seevers: 71.

[88] Kusy and Holloway, *Toxic Workplace!: Managing Toxic Personalities and Their Systems of Power*.

[89] Gregory S. McNeal, "Organizational Culture, Professional Ethics and Guantánamo," (Case Western Reserve University School of Law, 2010), 126.

[90] Goldman Alan, "Demagogue to Dialogue. An Alternative to Toxic Leadership in Corporate Downsizings," *Organizational Dynamics* 40, (2011); Goldman, *Transforming Toxic Leaders*; Kusy and Holloway, *Toxic Workplace!: Managing Toxic Personalities and Their Systems of Power*.

[91] Kusy and Holloway, *Toxic Workplace!: Managing Toxic Personalities and Their Systems of Power*, 71.

[92] Ibid.

[93] Ibid., 72.

[94] Jim Lehrer, "Online Newshour: Ralston Quits as Joint Chiefs Candidate", Duke Law Magazine http://www.law.duke.edu/lens/media/ralston.html.

[95] Barbara Kellerman, "How Bad Leadership Happens," *Leader to Leader* 2005, no. 35 (2005): 44.

[96] Padilla.

[97] Kusy and Holloway, *Toxic Workplace!: Managing Toxic Personalities and Their Systems of Power*.

[98] Padilla: 176.

[99] Samuel C. Rickless, "The Moral Status of Enabling Harm," *Pacific Philosophical Quarterly* 92, no. 1 (2011): 66.

[100] Kusy and Holloway, *Toxic Workplace!: Managing Toxic Personalities and Their Systems of Power*; Jean Lipman-Blumen, "The Allure of Toxic Leaders: Why Followers Rarely Escape Their Clutches," *Ivey Business Journal* 69, no. 3 (2005).

[101] P. Foot, "Morality, Action and Outcome," in *Morality and Objectivity: A Tribute to J. L. Mackie*, ed. T. Honderich(London: Routledge & Kegan Paul, 1985).

[102] Thoroughgood, Hunter, and Sawyer.

[103] Kusy and Holloway, *Toxic Workplace!: Managing Toxic Personalities and Their Systems of Power*.

[104] Ibid., 77.

[105] Warren Bennis, "Art of Followership," *Leadership Excellence* 27, no. 1 (2010): 3.

[106] L. R. Offerman, "When Followers Become Toxic," *Harvard Business Review* 1, (2004); Padilla.

[107] Bennis.

[108] Sims: 555.

[109] U.S. Department of the Army.

[110] H. Wells, "The Birth of Corporate Governance," *Seattle University Law Review* 33, no. 4 (2010).

[111] Hussein Tarraf, "The Role of Corporate Governance in the Events Leading up to the Global Financial Crisis: Analysis of Aggressive Risk-Taking," *Global Journal of Business Research* 5, no. 4 (2011): 95.

[112] Steele.

[113] Padilla: 186.

[114] Kusy and Holloway, *Toxic Workplace!: Managing Toxic Personalities and Their Systems of Power*, 15.

[115] Robert Debs Heinl, ed. *Dictionary of Military and Naval Quotations* (Annapolis,: United States Naval Institute, 1966), 245.

[116] Padilla.

[117] Ibid.

[118] Craig L. Pearce and others, "New Forms of Management: Shared and Distributed Leadership in Organizations," *Journal of Personnel Psychology* 9, no. 4 (2010): 152.